Published in the United States by Joka Heshima Jinsai and Abdul Olugbala Shakur

Printed in the United States of America.

ISBN: 9798831995947

Editor: Quaitie Stella Siverly

INDICTMENT OF THE STATE AND ITS PRISON INDUSTRIAL SLAVE COMPLEX

By: Joka Heshima Jinsai

Concept by: Abdul Olugbala Shakur

Table of Contents

PREAMBLE

The U.S. Racketeering, Influence and Corrupt Organizations Act, Title 18, Part I, Chapter 96 was initially enacted by Congress chiefly to combat the influence of organized criminal enterprises on the political, judicial and financial mechanisms of power in the U.S. The primary instrument used by those vested with the responsibility to prosecute such cases on behalf of the people is the indictment.

However, what do we do when the institutions responsible for upholding, and in some instances making, "the law" are the chief architects of its habitual violation? What do we, the People, do in an alleged "democracy" when the financial gain and political power of those who are vested with the responsibility of upholding the law is inextricably linked to maximizing the number of criminal offenders under their control; when their job security, livelihood, political and social influence is dependent on high crime and incarceration rates; when they are beholden to corporate interests in exchange for kickbacks and gratuities, to ensure profits are met on the backs of a constant flow of people being imprisoned?

This is the circumstance we as a society are faced with concerning the California Department of Corrections & rehabilitation, associated agencies and state administrators. The office of the Attorney General, in the normal course of affairs, would be the body vested with the responsibility of preparing, presenting and prosecuting such an indictment. However, the Attorney General is the Chief Counsel for CDCr and related officials, thus creating a conflict of interest which not only precludes them from objectively and competently pursuing such an indictment, but the merits of the indictment itself, historically speaking, tend to support their complicity in this criminal enterprise. As such, it falls to us, as servants of the people, to prepare this indictment on the people's behalf. The transformation of the U.S. prison system into the modern Prison Industrial Slave Complex (PISC) – and California's leading role in that process – is a study in the corrupting influence of money and political power on the very mechanisms of public safety. Though this particular indictment is focused on the California system (i.e., CDCr), it is our contention that this criminal enterprise is endemic of the modern PISC, and as such exists in every U.S. prison system. Therefore, this indictment can serve as a blueprint for the people to employ Nationally.

Title 18, s1961 defines "Racketeering Activity" in part as, "...any act or threat involving murder, kidnapping...robbery, bribery, extortion...dealing in controlled substances (or)...any act which is indictable under any...provision of Title 18." These indictable acts include offenses relating to everything from embezzlement to mail fraud, from slavery to the exploitation of children, and CDCr has presided over, or facilitated, all of these acts – and much, much more. The underlying basis of the following is founded on a readily observable, and fairly predictable, premise: the industrialization of human bondage in capitalist Amerika corrupted the instruments of "criminal justice" from the very outset. The biggest industry in the state of California is not agriculture, tourism, the technology of Silicon Valley or the movie industry in Hollywood — NO — its prisons. Just as slave plantations produced sugar and cotton to maintain agricultural and textile industries, prisons produce social control for political elites and corporate interests to continue the orderly extraction of labors surplus value (profit), contain nationally oppressed racial and ethnic groups and maintain the private appropriation of the social product (tax-dollar funded contracts). Prisons have been industrialized to the point where these interests have manufactured a new base of political support for this scheme: THE LABOR ARISTOCRACY OF PRISON GUARDS.

Prison guard "unions," like the California Correctional Peace Officers Association (CCPOA), wield a disproportionate amount of political influence in social life, all in support of the same political and corporate interests responsible for their relatively privileged position in the labor market.

The contemporary criminal justice system in Amerika is one of the biggest conflicts of interest in U.S. history. The system you've vested with the responsibility to ensure your public safety has their financial gain tied directly to the number of people "breaking the law" that they can hunt, catch, try, convict, sentence and imprison. Rehabilitation and public safety are not in their economic interests – criminalization and underdevelopment is.

This is a fairly simple equation: rehabilitation and social empowerment of offenders cannot be genuinely pursued because this would reduce the number of criminal offenders and parole violators, which would in turn decrease the need for so many police, lawyers, judges, deputies, jails, guards, prisons, and companies to support and supply them all – and most important of all – the need for your tax dollars to line their pockets. Public safety thus takes a backseat to personal gain. At the behest of the CCPOA lobbyists to bolster their bids for re-election, Legislators pass more laws and even stiffer penalties to broaden the net and deepen the pit for those who run afoul of "the law" to be cast into. Judges and lawyers continue to reinterpret the law to curtail Constitutional protections, civil liberties and access to the courts. Law enforcement sensationalize their "wars" on this or that type of crime to ensure you vote to pass bills and bond measures guaranteeing tougher laws, more militarized equipment, more police and more guards to inflate their already inflated budgets and salaries. District Attorneys maximize caseloads to ensure larger budgets and higher billings, while public defenders are forced to carry 25 cases at a time on shoestring budgets, reversing the burden of proof and effectively guaranteeing the conviction of low-income, overwhelmingly non-white offenders. Jails and prisons are overcrowded, underserved breeding grounds of racial violence, economic desperation and social despair. All of this, while the guards union lobbies for more prisons, harsher laws, more draconian judges and D.A.'s, better salaries and benefits, and finally, to convince you all that prisoners are irredeemable animals worthy of the perdition the state has created. Microsoft, Mead, Global Tel-Link, Frito Lay, Papermate, Walkenhorst, Mental Health Systems-Inc., Gregory Packaging, Inc., West Care, Bic, Walden House and hundreds of other corporations make hundreds of millions a year off of men, women, and children being locked up in California; a growth industry more lucrative than oil, and more corrupt than Chicago city government during prohibition.

Pursuing an indictment against individual offenders over the length and breadth of CDCr's history would not only be far too voluminous, but an act of futility, as it is the system itself which is corrupted. In case after case of proven criminal misconduct by CDCr officials and staff, individual offenders have pointed to their conduct as reflective of the department's policy(ies); "I was following my training" or "I was doing my job" has been repeatedly put forward as a cognizable defense to everything from facilitating rape, to acts of murder in the furtherance of an illegal gambling enterprise. This standard excuse serves to prove no matter who is standing in the warden's shoes, sitting in the IGI/ISU office, presiding over Juvenile Corrections or sitting in the Secretary of CDCr's chair, these corrupt practices are followed as a matter of "policy". This is the very definition of a racketeering enterprise; action with "intent to otherwise promote, manage, establish, carry on or facilitate promotion, management, establishment, or carrying on of any unlawful activity." It must be understood this is not a simple matter of poor correctional culture, this is a deliberate, well thought out racket presided over by law enforcement, correctional and political officials with billions of dollars in play and virtually no public oversight. In a culture that touts greed as a virtue, corruption under these conditions was a virtual certainty.

If there is to ever be any confidence in the integrity of the mechanisms of governance and public safety, the system itself must be indicted, its structural corruption exposed and alternative forms of social organization explored as a surer means of our collective security.

– Joka Heshima Jinsai

INDICTMENT PART 1

CONSPIRACY TO FACILITATE THE COMMISSION OF CRIMINAL ACTS VIA THE INTENTIONAL UNDERDEVELOPMENT OF BOTH WARDS CONFINED IN JUVENILE CORRECTIONS AND THE INTENTIONAL FAILURE TO REHABILITATE ADULT OFFENDERS.

Because these acts and omissions constitute the deliberate promotion of criminal activity as a means to leverage ever increasing shares of the general taxpayer fund in order to enrich themselves, their corporate conspirators and their political proxies constituting racketeering activity on behalf of the California Department of Corrections & rehabilitation. CDCr controls every aspect of programming and opportunity for development and rehabilitation for the Prisoners committed to their custody and have presided over the intentional underdevelopment and conscious denial of opportunities for viable educational development and job skills training for CDCr Prisoners. Such underdevelopment and lack of rehabilitation, particularly as it relates to presiding over conditions designed to maximize recidivism, is evidence of the specific intent of correctional officials to maximize property, service-based and predatory crimes (i.e. robbery, extortion, murder, etc.). That such willful criminal facilitation is specifically intended to maximize incarceration rates and drive social support for the carceral state, and in turn ensure the maximization of salaries, benefits and job security for correctional officers and officials, constitutes an ongoing illicit enterprise with the specific intent of criminally misappropriating taxpayer dollars.

Because this criminal enterprise is interconnected to so many other racketeering activities it is particularly egregious as the acts and omissions by correctional officers and officials have become institutionalized, corrupting the political and legislative institutions in the state. The totality of these acts and omissions constitute the deliberate facilitation of robbery, murder, kidnapping, dealing in (and use of) controlled substances, burglary, petty theft and a plethora of other criminal offenses as a means to leverage ever increasing shares of the general fund to enrich themselves, their corporate conspirators and their political proxies. As such, these criminal acts constitute a pattern of racketeering activity, municipal financial institution fraud, and unlawful payments to a labor organization in violation of Title 18 U.S.C. 1961 (A) and (B), s1344, s1952 and Title 29 U.S.C. 186. Each correctional officer is, or has been, a member of the California Correctional Peace Officers Association (CCPOA) Guards Union at some point in their career. The CCPOA collectively bargains for the exorbitant salaries and benefits for all CDCr officers. These generous salaries (the highest of any corrections department in the U.S.) ensure the maintenance of high union dues. Those dues are then used to influence political, judicial and legislative appointments, elections, policies and processes which favor CDCr interests in maintaining – or increasing – those luxurious salaries and benefits, and their numbers. This in turn further strengthens the CCPOA and CDCr, as well as their corporate/political cabal. None of this would be possible without a plausible and politically "legitimate" reason for the virtually unfettered access to the taxpayer General Fund accorded CDCr. The intentional facilitation and maintenance of criminal recidivism and the subsequent (manufactured) "threat" to public safety it poses, is the "reason" employed to affect this systematic criminal misappropriation; a reason of CDCr's own making. The duration of these offenses are so extensive and long standing, spanning the administrations and tenures of CDCr Directors, Secretaries, wardens – and their administration – and rank & file officers dating back over 100 years, that the number of individual counts and defendants involved would be far too voluminous to list here. As such, it is our contention that this criminal enterprise is institutional, and has become effectively systematic where by all prison officials and officers, no matter who may be currently occupying the Directors' office, Secretaries' chair, wardens' office, or custody staffs' position are willfully engaged in a pattern of racketeering activity reasonably concluded to import otherwise preventable crime into our communities via the intentional failure to vocationally/educationally develop and rehabilitate Prisoners, and thus threatening the life, liberty and property of Prisoners and the public, for their political and financial gain.

INDICTMENT COUNT 1:

INTENTIONAL CREATION OF RECIDIVISM TO ENSURE HIGH INCARCERATION RATES AND PRISON POPULATIONS.

In the state of California, the prison population has risen by 800% since 1985. These massive prison populations in turn serve to maintain corporate contracts with supply, service and prison firms at profitable levels for these corporations, who in turn ensure kickbacks and other financial and/or political considerations to the department, its officials and political proxies. As demonstrated earlier in Part 1, CDCr has historically underfunded, withheld or discontinued resources and presided over conditions specifically designed to undermine rehabilitation and viable job skills training for Prisoners to ensure those released would return to prison. Simultaneously, CDCr has utilized its undue political influence in the legislature and the press to successfully lobby for draconian mandatory minimums, harsher sentences for already existing offenses and the creation of new laws to criminalize conduct which was previously not a crime, all with the intent of expanding the prison industry in the state and their share of the general fund to maximize the financial gain of its officers and administrators, in violation of racketeering statutes.

There exists extensive evidence that CDCr is actively colluding in this criminal enterprise with corporate entities who provide kickbacks and financial/political considerations to CDCr officials and interests (i.e. CCPOA) in exchange for awarded contracts to provide goods, services, supplies, maintenance, and in the case of private contractors, bed space for prisoners. Kickbacks and gratuities have taken the form of contributions to pro-incarceration judges, politicians and legislatures: donations to the guards union; payment "reimbursements" to specific prison administrations, and other gifts. These arrangements have taken the form of everything from overpayments to contractors, to paying full price for "irregular" goods and food items which are in actuality discounted, allowing providers and the Department to split the difference of the allocated funds. These corrupt relationships ensure the conditions for recidivism in the Department remain high; public opposition to the passage of draconian laws and the over criminalization of New Afrikans, Latinos and poor communities remains low, and their exploitation of taxpayer dollars for their own financial gain remains constant and unmolested. Prisoners are charged exorbitant prices for goods and services which are much less expensive for the same, and even more valuable, goods and services in the broader economy. This arrangement constitutes a virtual monopoly in this captive market by a few handpicked vendors who financially support the interests of state prison officials and their political proxies. This level of corruption, and intentional criminalization in the service of incarceration, for the financial gain of departmental employees and related corporate interests constitutes a pattern of racketeering, engaging in monetary transactions in property derived from specific unlawful activity, usury, municipal financial institution fraud, and the corruption of civil servants in violation of Title 18s1,Chapter 96 (R.I.C.O. Act), s1961, s1344; Title 29 U.S.C. S186 and related federal state laws and statutes.

INDICTMENT COUNT 2:

INTENTIONALLY CREATING A SYSTEM IN CALIFORNIA YOUTH AUTHORITY (CYA) AND PRIVATE YOUTH FACILITIES TO DEVELOP ULTRA-VIOLENT, SEXUALLY ABUSIVE, HYPER-VIGILANT, EDUCATIONALLY UNDERDEVELOPED YOUNG PEOPLE; PREDOMINANTLY NEW AFRIKAN, LATINO AND POOR, TO FUEL BOTH YOUTH AND ADULT RECIDIVISM AND INCARCERATION RATES.

This empirical and case study evidence demonstrates CDCr, in conjunction with judicial, legislative and corporate partners are presiding over the systemic criminalization and imprisonment of underprivileged children and intentionally hardwiring their core psychology to re-offend, often violently, as a matter of course, then releasing them back into communities with no education, vocational or job prospects, knowing full well they will do what the state trained them to do; survive by any means necessary.

To fully understand the scope of Count 2 of the indictment, we must analyze the process and purpose of these acts and omissions to clearly illuminate their criminal intent. Survival in New Afrikan, Latino, poor and other oppressed communities in the U.S. are a study in psychological stress, perpetual socio-economic uncertainty/insecurity and genuine fear (i.e. fear of police, violent death, hunger, homelessness, joblessness, eviction, child neglect, drug addiction, domestic violence, etc.) giving rise to constant assaults on the nervous equipment and neurological-chemical development of children in these communities. The unfortunate, but not unexpected, result is most children in these communities suffer from psychological disorders and structural alterations in the distinct physiology of their brains, which drastically reduces impulse control and impedes rational thought. Manifestations of these psychological and neurological injuries in highly policed and socially contained communities have often run contrary to the "law," many times in conjunction with prohibited survival activities and (misguided) attempts at social empowerment; i.e. drug trafficking, gang activity, etc. All too often, these children land in juvenile hall and ultimately child prison, known in this state as the California Youth Authority, or CYA.

It is here in CYA, and similar youth penal systems across America, where the process of warping these children's minds for the implicit economic and political gain of the Department and its partners becomes overtly criminal. Definitively addressing the underlying socio-economic disparities in underclass communities, or at least providing comprehensive treatment for the mental damage inflicted on these children by the current order of property relations, has never been considered by the state as a serious alternative to imprisoning children. The U.S. is one of the only industrialized western nations which has not signed the U.N. Rights of the Child Treaty which prohibits the imprisonment of children, and California's CYA is a prime example of why the treaty exists. The institutions which comprise the CYA, like Nellis and Y.T.S. (Youth Training System), are much more violent and predatory than adult institutions, and youth consigned to them are trained to be as violent as their environment in order to simply survive. Corporal punishment, the use of restraint chairs, the use of solitary confinement and non-consensual psychiatric medication (often in conjunction with restraints) are common practices in CYA facilities.

These state sponsored torture techniques have the objective effect of maximizing the psychological and anti-social impact of the conditions in the CYA facilities themselves. It is the assessment of our analysis that the very policy foundations of CYA and youth correctional facilities, the way they are structured, run and managed – by design – produce ultra-violent, socially underdeveloped, human time-bombs which are knowingly released back into the community with no educational or vocational development prospects, certainly no therapy or counseling, and no hope, other than what the state has taught them in these institutions. In CYA, there are only two types of prisoners: predators and prey. You either fight to get and maintain your "respect," or you become someone's "case," a submissive who pays for 'protection' with whatever he/she has. This servitude includes, in some cases, vile sexual submission, where the bodies and minds of these children are subjected to even more debased forms of torture: RAPE.

According to the 2008-09 California Justice Statistics Report on Incarceration, the sexual assault rate in CYA was 9.6%, 3 times higher than that in adult prisons. However, it was the Attorney General's belief that the number of sexual assaults in male youth facilities could be significantly higher, since female Prisoners were 6 times more likely to report rape by fellow wards or staff than their male counterparts. The resultant physical and psychological damage for both victims and (in the case of child perpetrators) aggressors, from HIV exposure to acute emotional and psychological trauma, bode ill for behavior after release. Hypervigilance, bordering on manic paranoia, becomes the primary mode of thought for these children, under the Department's stewardship. Carrying a weapon becomes the survival norm, as essential to life in the minds of these youth as breathing. Gang life in CYA institutions often meant continued life, and concentrated racism is enforced by the very arrangement of these facilities, all with the full knowledge and consent of staff.

According to CYA Custody Counselor R. Rodriguez's testimony in People v. Colbert, in 2004 the California Youth Authority boasted a 91% recidivism rate, and these recidivism levels had been the norm for years. According to his testimony, educational and vocational development of wards was a far removed consideration among CYA staff as their primary concern was to secure incarceration and violence management. Their methods prove their criminal intent. Youth Correctional staff in CYA facilities routinely designate places called "blinds" where children can fight one another and staff don't have to intervene and do "unnecessary" paperwork. In other cases, staff has sponsored the blood sport, like the infamous "Friday Night Fights" staff held with young wards at Paso, pitting rival wards against one another in after hour fights, arranged on staff's "fight cards". When wards did not cease fighting when staff called round "over," they would beat the non-compliant child(ren) into submission with a wooden mace. Drugs, alcohol, tobacco and other contraband are routinely introduced by staff to select child prisoners to reward enforcement of staff dictates – or simply for money.

In spite of tacking on an "R" (for Rehabilitation) to the end of CDC, genuine attempts to intervene and develop these children to their ultimate potential in a clean, safe environment are non-existent in juvenile corrections. The very idea of CDCr providing *genuine* rehabilitation is in fact a running joke amongst Prisoners. Educational and vocational programs are underfunded, understaffed and outdated. Educational and vocational programs are marginalized in favor of "incarceration only" policies on the ground. The Corrections Department is fully cognizant of the nature and structure of the system it put into place. It is a genius, if insidious, equation: The CCPOA

(California Correctional Peace Officers Association) is the largest and most powerful lobbying force in the state, and its members have unrestrained power over how youth (and adult) correctional institutions are run. They subject children within these institutions – deliberately during the formative years of their brains – to these brutal and abusive environments for years at a time (most of them already psychologically damaged) and warp their minds beyond recognition.

They then release them back into society, ill-equipped to navigate social life and uneducated beyond the rewiring of their minds provided by this "prison training" (YTS: Youth Training System) knowing full well they will resort to that indoctrination to survive in U.S. capitalist society. When newly released youth offenders follow this predictable training and reoffend, prison industrialists and their partners in law enforcement, political office and mass media will point to these youth and extol why imprisonment is the only sure cure for "violent criminals," totally suppressing the fact that they've painstakingly cultivated these youth to do just this. The Department conveniently washes their hands of their own culpability in one tragedy after another with the tears of the victim's and offenders families alike. They conscientiously gather that same anger and resentment in society (with the aid of mass media) and heap it on the heads of their unwitting tools (former Prisoners) with one hand, and with the other they dip deeper into the purses and pockets of taxpayers for more of their dollars to secure higher salaries, hire more guards, build more prisons, to have more prisoners, to justify the need for even MORE tax dollars from the general fund; a self-perpetuating racketeering enterprise involving acts of and threats of assault, murder, kidnapping, gambling, trafficking controlled substances – and people, financial institution fraud, sexual exploitation of children, illegal payments to labor organizations, criminal influence in legislation (i.e. ALEC), undue criminal influence in political affairs (i.e. CCPOA), all built on the backs, blood and broken minds of thousands of children. Through these illegal acts and omissions CDCr maintains the PISC's imperative to perpetuate and expand itself at the expense of already besieged communities and public safety. Those responsible for the development of this criminal enterprise (CDCr) have eluded culpability, because they've succeeded in duping the nation into becoming unconscious co-conspirators in the dehumanization and exploitation of children from New Afrikan, Latino (Latinx) and poor communities. It must be understood that this is as a pattern and practice of criminal conduct within the Department, based on the vestiges of slavery, Jim Crow law and an economic ideology stretching in a direct historical line from 1619 to the present day; an economic ideology so prevalent and widespread that it is (now) the custom and policy of the Department and related institutions encompassing every prison administrator, custody staff supervisor, staff member and employee enriched in this scheme, making the citation of individual offenders far too voluminous for this document.

To be sure, in each case where criminal conduct was exposed in concert, such as Prison Guards in Corcoran SHU going on trial for setting up their own "Blood Sport" style fights on the SHU yard, then fatally shooting Prisoners they lost bets on, Prison Guards were subsequently acquitted because it was "the policy", not them, that was responsible for their actions, and "the policy" came from Sacramento (the state capitol) so they were "just following their training." A similar argument made by Nazi era guards at Auschwitz during the Nuremberg trials. In any case, it is the Department and state itself responsible for these crimes, AND every employee involved in the illicit activity. When a psychologically damaged child is intentionally treated like an animal throughout their developmental years, and repeatedly told they are a "criminal," then does what they were trained by the state to do, the agency which purposely made them that way must be held accountable. Is there any wonder why the recidivism rate in CYA was 91%? Companies and lobbies like GEO Group, Smith Barney, Mental Health Systems, Walkenhorst, the CCPOA and so many others are getting richer and more powerful off the tax dollars and votes elicited by this criminal racket, while making certain public safety remains perpetually jeopardized.

The youth from these underdeveloped communities have become a means to an end in an economic and political arrangement where children are reduced to mere commodities the Department can warehouse, train, release and re-warehouse in "Prisoner Factories" whose economic potential is only limited by the number of human commodities they have under their control at any given point. In such a criminal enterprise the objective acts of torture, suborning rape, assault, gang violence, drug use, drug (and human) trafficking, truancy and intentional educational underdevelopment under the doctrine of causation, of course, are indictable. That this pattern of racketeering activity is being carried out for financial gain and political influence at the expense of children is particularly heinous. It is our contention that the willful failure to pursue a course of action which would at least limit, if not eliminate, youth criminalization coupled with CDCr's intentional distortion of the material facts surrounding their culpability in intentionally perpetuating this criminalization, represents consciousness of guilt in this criminal enterprise. This level of corruption and intentional criminalization of children constitutes a particularly vile and evil intent on the part of the Department's employees and related corporate/political interests, much akin to the raising of child soldiers, in parts of war torn Africa. This pattern of racketeering, fraud and corruption of public institutions stands in direct violation of Title 18, Part 1, Chapter 16 (R.I.C.O Act), Title 18 s1961 (1) (A & B), s1344, s1952, s2260 and Title 29, U.S.C. S186.

INDICTMENT PART II

ACTS OF DIRECT RACKETEERING ACTIVITY IN PRISON BY CDC(r) OFFICIALS.

INDICTMENT COUNT 3:

ASSAULT.

CDC(r) employees have knowingly and intentionally engaged in a pattern of physical assaults on Prisoners, both with and without firearms, and directly engaged in orchestrating assaults on individuals and groups of Prisoners by other Prisoners acting as proxies – most often racial attacks against New Afrikan (Black) Prisoners – in a pattern of violence carried out under color of law specifically designed to deprive those subject to those assaults of their most basic Constitutional protections under the 1st, 8th and 14th Amendments U.S.C. in furtherance of a criminal enterprise.

Over the course of CDCr's tenure there have been numerous instances of assaults on Prisoners by staff and assaults of Prisoners orchestrated by staff, some so politically repressive, massively brutal or particularly debased, that they've taken on historic significance. These instances of assaults are so numerous, and the names of individual perpetrators so voluminous, that listing each individual act is beyond the scope of this indictment. However, the instances of officer led and/or officer orchestrated assaults are so common that for purposes of this indictment we will recount some of the most significant types of assaults that have been carried out in furtherance of this criminal enterprise.

CDCr officers and officials, most often in retaliation for some perceived slight or perceived threat by a Prisoner, have:

- Assembled "teams" of 5 or more officers (and at times including administrators) to "Teach [a Prisoner] their place."

- Assembled "teams" of 5 or more officers (and at times officials) near a targeted Prisoner's cell, have the cell opened and enter en masse and beat the Prisoner(s) in question until they are satisfied. Then that Prisoner will be placed in Ad-seg (the hole) and charged with "assaulting staff" while "delaying a Peace Officer in the commission of his/her duties."

- Prisoners from different racial groups or street organizations (i.e. Southern Mexican & White Prisoners vs. New Afrikan (Black) Prisoners; Crips vs. Bloods, etc., etc.) will be intentionally pit against each other; especially in instances where Prisoners' unity led to organized resistance to inhumane conditions is present, or perceived to be present, by staff (most often led by New African (Black) Prisoners and animosities between street or prison based organizations, to ensure Prisoners remain focused primarily on attacking one another, and not resisting the inhumane policies and conditions of the Prison Industrial Slave Complex.

- CDCr staff have on multiple occasions armed White and Mexican Prisoners, or allowed them to maintain their weapons, after doing mass searches to confiscate actual and potential weapons from New Afrikan (Black) Prisoners, the orchestrated conditions which allowed the two sides to assault one another, with White or

Mexican Prisoners being armed, while New Afrikan Prisoners were unarmed.

- During instances of racial conflict, while doing controlled movement, CDC(r) staff have routinely opened the cell doors of a Prisoner(s) from one group, while a large number of an opposing group were on the tier, and allowed them to run into that Prisoner's cell and assault them.

- During racial conflicts, being that the vast majority of CDC(r) staff are White or Mexican, they often sided with those Prisoners from their cultural group(s). There have been numerous instances where white or Mexican Prisoners would attack New Afrikans (Blacks) in the chow hall, and when the New Afrikans Prisoners would respond in self-defense (often effectively) the attacking Whites or Mexicans would get down and the gun tower staff would shoot the New Afrikan. This was so wide-spread at one point it became a standard tactic.

- CDC(r) staff in Ad-seg and SHU facilities have repeatedly orchestrated gladiator style fights at multiple institutions for entertainment purposes, financial gain (gambling) and to ensure the perpetuation of rivalries between racial groups and/or Prisoner/Street Organizations. Prisoners from different and opposing factions would be intentionally let into the exercise yard for the purpose of assaulting one another for the pleasure of the guards. In many instances where gambling between staff on the outcomes did not go in the favor of specific staff, they would shoot the offending victor.

- In Ad-seg and SHU facilities, in those instances where staff feel as though they may have been slighted, offended or otherwise "disrespected" they will wait until the particular Prisoner is being escorted to or from medical, showers, law library, etc. where they must submit to mechanical restraints and close the cuffs on their wrists to injure them, yank the chain as they're being escorted, or trip the Prisoner so they fall with no way to catch themselves. When the Prisoner moves to protest this treatment, staff assaults the Prisoner with chemical agents (pepper spray, mace, etc.) or simply beats them with fists and clubs. To ensure official sanction is given to the assault, staff compounds the crime with another, by falsifying a fictitious rules violation report alleging, "Resisting a Peace Officer resulting in use of force" or "Assault on staff."

- In numerous instances in SHU and Ad-seg, CDC(r) staff has opened the doors of rival Prisoners while opposing Prisoners are on the tier (intentionally), allowing Prisoners to assault one another. In other instances, too numerous to name, they have facilitated 2 on 1 scenarios where one Prisoner must defend himself against two attackers.

- In numerous instances CDC(r) staff has used Tasers, electric stun belts, Billy clubs, mace, pepper spray, high velocity water hoses and other weapons to assault Prisoners they've targeted for personal, political or other illegitimate reason(s).

- Staff have repeatedly used sexual assault (rape) as a form of "corporal punishment" against Prisoners who (in most instances are physically small), they feel have been "disrespectful" towards staff. In numerous cases, both in Ad-seg/SHU and general population facilities, staff have intentionally moved or transferred offending Prisoners who they feel may have been verbally abusive or assaultive towards a staff member, (most often young, physically small Prisoners) into the cell with documented violent sexual predators known as "booty bandits" to be beaten and raped repeatedly – often for days, weeks or even months on end – while staff ignore the screams and knowingly allow the abuse to continue.

- In numerous instances where Prisoners are active litigants or organizers in protests against such oppressive prison conditions, or have led strikes or protests against such inhumane conditions, state actors have repeatedly targeted them for assault by other Prisoners who may be rivals of their cultural or organizational group, simply at the behest of staff, in exchange for some gratuity or consideration. These attempted assassinations and violent coercive attacks are particularly heinous as they seek to freeze 1st Amendment speech and/or access to the courts, and is particularly designed to retaliate against those who seek to positively change the conditions of imprisonment.

We could list more, as the variation in circumstances for unlawful assaults on Prisoners carried out by, or presided over, by CDC(r) staff is virtually infinite in furtherance of this criminal enterprise; but this list is sufficiently representative of CDC(r) acts and omissions for purposes of this count in the indictment. This pattern and practice of assaults in support of an ongoing racketeering enterprise stands in violation of 18 U.S.C. S1959, s1961, s1962, R.I.C.O. Act, P.C. 187, P.C. 186.2 and P.C. 13519.6.

INDICTMENT COUNT 4:

MURDER.

CDC(r) employees have knowingly and intentionally engaged in a pattern of murder in continuance of a criminal enterprise which has included facilitating murders by prisoner proxies, creating conditions to afford the opportunity to commit murder under the color of law, and committing murder through willful medical neglect and/or withholding medical care.

The commission, or facilitation, of murders by CDC(r) have been carried out primarily to repress organized resistance by Prisoners against abuses, inhumane Prison conditions or to prevent exposure to the public of this ongoing criminal enterprise by Prisoner litigants and/or political/politicized Prisoners. This means the primary purpose of murders carried out, or facilitated by CDC(r) staff, were/are to dissuade, retaliate against or freeze the speech of Prisoners they consider(ed) to be a threat – or potential threat – to their ongoing racketeering operations (i.e., perpetuation of the P.I.S.C.). Secondarily, it's purpose is to kill those Prisoners who staff find offensive or are in opposition to particular groups which may be favored by the staff in question, through protracted means (i.e., racism, personal animosity, siding with particular groups against others in gang or race based conflicts, etc., etc.). These instances of murder, or the facilitation of murder, are again so numerous in nature, spanning over a century, and the list of perpetrators so voluminous that citing every individual case extends well beyond the scope of this indictment. Instead, we will recount some of the most common types and infamous cases of murder CDC(r) employees have carried out, or facilitated, over the span of its tenure, to serve as a representation of the totality of these criminal acts.

- In numerous instances CDC(r) staff has fomented conflicts between rival racial groups and/or organizations to create conditions which would allow staff members to assassinate a targeted Prisoner or group of Prisoners. In most of these instances staff would target New Afrikan Revolutionary Nationalist (N.A.R.N.) Prisoners. Be it on the tier or prison yard, CDC(r) staff would release white supremacists and/or rival Mexican Prisoners specifically to attack N.A.R.N. Prisoners, and when New Afrikan Prisoners would meet the attacks with self-defense, or see the set-up and seek to pre-empt it, colluding staff in the gun towers would shoot and kill the targeted New Afrikan Prisoner(s). This is not to say this assassination tactic was used exclusively against New Afrikan Prisoners, but this tactic was used most often on New Afrikan Prisoners who were often at the forefront of anti-Prison Industrialization protests or litigation against prison conditions and/or abusive employees.

- In multiple instances staff would assemble outside a targeted Prisoner's cell and enter with 3 or more staff to assault the Prisoner, who often fought back against the beatings. Once beaten unconscious, staff would fashion a noose out of his/her sheet or other material and hang the prisoner from the vent, light, top bunk or other fixture, put the cell back in order then leave. Hours later staff would walk the tier and "discover" the targeted Prisoner dead from an "apparent suicide." Because the perpetrators actually process the scene and issue the circumstances under which the victim was discovered to the coroner, very rarely, if ever, has there been any investigation into these "suicide" style murders.

- In multiple instances where Prisoners are engaged in a simple fist fight or altercation (again, most often New Afrikan Prisoners), staff in the gun tower will tell them to "get down," and the Prisoners will comply. It will then be the tower staff (in many cases a known racist), when seeing them proned out, will target a particular Prisoner and still shoot him in the back, chest or head, killing them for no obvious reason outside of racial or political animus.

- In multiple instances staff in the gun tower (who either hold some animosity towards a particular Prisoner and/or group of Prisoners, or who identifies with a rival group or organization of a particular Prisoner or group of Prisoners) will open the cell door of a targeted Prisoner and allow rival Prisoners to enter their cell and murder them. On other occasions the targeted Prisoner may be on the tier, and the tower staff will open the doors of the rival Prisoners and let them murder the targeted Prisoner on the tier, in some instances aiding them by shooting the victim as he's being stabbed and/or trying to defend himself.

- In multiple instances staff has knowingly released a targeted Prisoner into the exercise yard of a rival racial group or opposing organization and then turn away, allowing the targeted Prisoner to be murdered.

- In multiple instances CDC(r) staff would take sides in racial or organizational conflicts, arming their proxies with explosives, bomb-making material, guns, ammunition, knives, hacksaw blades and metal stock to produce homemade firearms, knives, bombs and other weapons to kill rival Prisoners. This logistical support resulted in the murders of numerous Prisoners, and served as a potent political and legislative tool for the California Correctional Peace Officers Association (CCPOA), as well, pointing to the escalating violence and increasing death rates as "proof of the incorrigible nature of offenders" and need for harsher sentencing, more laws, more prison guards and new prison construction. CDC(r) was able to secure for itself a much larger share of public dollars (i.e. expanded budgets, higher salaries, more benefits, etc.). Using their complete control of the narrative, CDC(r) has used these opportunities to scapegoat visiting friends and family of Prisoners as the source of contraband weapons, knowing full well it is virtually impossible to smuggle in guns, metal of any kind, explosives, or other weapons material into prisons through visiting, and was/is in fact almost always staff providing such weapons and material to Prisoners.

- In multiple instances, staff would collude with a rival racial group or organization of Prisoners to set up an ambush-style assassination on a targeted Prisoner. In these instances, staff would allow groups of armed proxies to lie in wait in a particular part of the prison that could be quickly closed off, such as a sally port or rotunda, and direct the targeted Prisoner to report to a location that would take them through the ambush point. Once in position, the staff would close the doors, trapping the target in the confined space of the ambush site where they would be murdered.

- In multiple instances, staff has set up gladiator-style fights between Prisoners from rival groups or organizations in Ad-seg and SHU units for both illegal gambling and political purposes (manufacturing Prisoner violence statistics, etc.). In those instances where the "wrong" Prisoner prevailed or staff is upset at the outcome, the targeted Prisoner was shot and killed.

- In multiple instances CDC(r) staff have intentionally withheld or delayed the delivery of necessary medical care or emergency first aid in order to murder critically injured or chronically ill Prisoners. In multiple instances where Prisoners have been shot, injured or chronically ill (often targeted New Afrikan Political Prisoners or other Political prisoners) staff have withheld emergency medical intervention until they have bled out or intentionally neglected to provide appropriate medical care for other injuries and/or illnesses (i.e. head injury, heart attack, stroke, pneumonia, diabetic shock, etc.) until they have died. This practice is so common and widespread that intentional medical neglect or delayed care resulted in the death of two Prisoners per week on average, prompting CDC(r) health care services to be placed into medical receivership by the courts.

We could list more, as CDC(r) has over the decades murdered and facilitated the murder of targeted prisoners in an almost infinite number of ways in furtherance of their ongoing criminal enterprise. However, what's presented here is sufficiently representative of CDC(r)'s acts and omissions over the decades to clearly evidence a pattern of murder in furtherance of a racketeering enterprise.

These murders, like the countless murders before them, were carried out to further CDC(r)'s racketeering activity by intimidating other Prisoners from opposing the status quo of inhumane conditions or pursuing litigation and/or protest against the department's abuses. Such action could also intimidate the families of Prisoners, or mislead the public as to the true nature of this violence, thus inhibiting them from pursuing public opposition to, or reform of, the Prison Industrial Slave Complex. In this context, these murders have an equally adverse impact on the state of California's, and the Nation's interest in maintaining humane, corruption-free prisons and the free enjoyment and protection of our constitutional rights. This pattern and practice of murder in support of an ongoing racketeering enterprise stand in violation of 18 U.S.C. S1959, s1961, s1962, the RICO Act, P.C. S187, P.C. S186.2 and P.C. S13519.6.

INDICTMENT COUNT 5:

CONSPIRACY TO MAINTAIN A DOMESTIC TORTURE PROGRAM.

CDCr employees have engaged in a pattern and practice of systematic torture to coerce information, suppress politically progressive ideas and attitudes, and do permanent psychological damage to targeted Prisoners.

CDC(r) has maintained a domestic torture program in "dungeon" cells, "strip" cells and SHU units (security housing units) for well over a century. The primary function of the program is to inflict such continuous physical and psychological torture, pain, and suffering on those subject to these units that their minds actually "break," and they either submit completely to the dictates of the state (i.e. CDCr) – no matter how contrary to their interests or basic human rights those dictates may be – go mad, or in the case of those who resist indefinitely, to serve as living examples to the rest of the Prisoner population of the state's absolute power over their bodies, much as crucifixions served the Romans.

In the case of the "dungeon" cells, Prisoners would be stripped naked and forced into a urine and feces covered stone cell with no light, a hole in the floor as a toilet, no running water and nothing else but the stench and the darkness. A bare mattress would be issued at last count and taken away again first thing in the morning. No linen or clothing were provided in these cold, dank and filthy stone boxes because CDCr employees wanted to ensure Prisoners were subject to the perpetual indignity of nakedness, and could not escape through suicide.

The department's regulations and state law on "dungeon" cells stipulated that, "Prisoners shall not be housed for more than 10 days" inside one. However, for those who maintained their dignity, sanity and principles (characterized as "defiant" by staff), or depending on the level of sadism staff on that watch expressed, Prisoners were frequently removed from the "dungeon" cell and placed in a holding cage for one hour on the 10th day, then put back into the "dungeon" cell for another 10. In the most severe use of this torture chamber, one subject (a New Afrikan Revolutionary Nationalist) was confined there for a record six (6) months. The physical and psychological toll of such torture chambers is so severe, the isolation so intense and contrary to human mental wellness, that many simply went mad.

The introduction of Security Housing Units (SHU's) into Old Folsom and San Quentin Adjustment Center (AC) was the precursor to California's modern torture units at Pelican Bay, Corcoran and elsewhere. These units, in contrast to the medieval brutality of the "dungeon" cells, were clinically designed to break men's minds and export the "informant psychosis" to their communities. The conceptual framework for the SHU design finds its origins in a meeting of prison wardens and social scientists held in Washington D.C. in 1962. There Dr. Edgar Schein delivered his findings in a speech titled, "Man Against Man: Brainwashing" and the concept of the modern 'Supermax Control Unit' was born.

In addressing the group Dr. Schein stated: "I would like you to think of brainwashing not in terms of politics, ethics or morals, but in terms of the deliberate changing of human behavior and attitudes by a group of men who have relatively complete control over the environment in which the captive populace lives." Its political intent was clear from the outset. Former Warden Ralph Aron of one of the first supermax lock-up units, Marion Supermax, stated the purpose of the SHU's was "to control Revolutionary attitudes in the prison system and society at large." What Dr. Schein and his cohorts provided was its function.

To be effective, the new techniques he described would require a new type of environment, one which could alter the very foundations of one's perception of reality. For this they would adopt Dr. Levinson's sensory deprivation Prison Unit design and a form of Skinnerian operant conditioning called "Learned Helplessness." This last technique is a key factor in the California State Domestic Torture Program in both its "validation" based indeterminate SHU confinement and "debriefing" process. "Learned Helplessness" is a systemic process of conditioning designed to crystallize in the imprisoned victim's mind that he or she has no control over the regulation of his/her existence, that they are completely dependent on the state and it's guards for the necessities of "life"; that he/she is helpless and must submit to the state's power and control in order to "survive."

Because this type of forced submission runs contrary to human consciousness, a linear thought divergence occurs into two options: RESISTANCE or ESCAPE. The program is designed to apply maximum punitive coercion against "resistance" from the outset: physical removal from general population and confinement to solitary, sensory deprivation, utilization of informants, collaborators and agent provocateurs to erode trust amongst those in like circumstances, punishing uncooperative attitudes, prohibiting collective thought and expression, while simultaneously employing group punishment, punitive property restrictions, arbitrary punishment, etc., etc.

Those capable of indefinite resistance through ideological/political development or force of will, like victims of crucifixion left to rot on crosses during the Roman Empire, served as powerful deterrents to those of lesser psychological resistance. These less developed subjects in SHU, or those still in general population, confronted with the ever present specter of indefinite SHU confinement were conditioned to avoid resistance, and instead explored the second option: ESCAPE.

Though Marion Control Unit was among the first prisons in the Schein-Levinson-Skinnerian Torture System, the most infamous by far is California's premier control unit: Pelican Bay SHU. Because one of the central functions of these new control units was to leverage torture to coerce information from its victims, Pelican Bay SHU made its "escape" option clear: "Parole, Debrief or DIE."

As a result of the undue influence of the PISC on the legislative, political – and to a degree – cultural apparatus of the state (and Nation), most validated SHU Prisoners are serving mandatory minimums, enhanced sentences or Board of Prison Terms (BPT) based indeterminate terms, and their very confinement in the SHU is prohibitive to their parole: "If you want a parole date, you probably want to think about debriefing," is a common statement from Parole Board governors to SHU prisoners before them. This increases the psychological pressure on those already weakened by the conviction that they've been abandoned by, and isolated from, society, and only through submission and subservience can they be socially accepted as human beings.

This form of "escape," known as "Debriefing" (in essence becoming an informant or agent of the state), is consistent with points 7, 8 and 9 of Dr. Schein's behavior modification method: "(7) Exploration of opportunities; (8) Convincing Prisoners they can trust no one; (9) Treating those who are willing to collaborate in far more lenient ways than those who are not." That beatings, assaults, gladiator style matches and murder are also liberally employed in SHU torture units only exacerbates the attacks on the nervous equipment of those subject to indefinite solitary confinement.

That indefinite or even relatively short-term solitary confinement constitutes torture is undeniable, and something the U.S., and the state of California, have known since the 1870's (see In Re Medeley). However, with lobbying efforts by guard unions, like California's C.C.P.O.A., and the nationwide march towards the expansion of control units we've witnessed over the previous 30 years, the clinical approach to domestic torture has taken on an almost Auschwitz style tone in its matter of fact use.

Title 18 U.S.C. s2340 and U.N. Convention Against Torture, Article I, section 2 defines "Torture" as "Any act by which severe pain or suffering, whether physical or mental, is intentionally inflicted on a person for such purposes as obtaining from him/her or a third person, information or a confession, punishing him/her for an act he/she or a third party has committed or is suspected of having committed, or intimidating or coercing a third person." This definition is synonymous with the purpose and function of California's SHU units, and supermax control units across the nation. That the U.S. has preserved for itself a "legal exemption" for domestic torture has no bearing on its criminal nature (Title 18 s2340 is enforceable only outside the U.S., so any acts of torture as defined in s2340 committed within the U.S. are not crimes under U.S. law, unless they are accompanied by severe physical injury). Torture is a crime. Coercion through torture to elicit information to further a criminal enterprise is a greater crime. Leveraging scientists, psychologists and structural engineers to methodically strip away the minds and humanity of captive victims to transform them into active tools of the state is evil.

Conceptually intended for exclusive use on politically progressive Prisoners (i.e. Imprisoned Black Panther Party, Amerikan Indian Movement, Weather Underground, Black Guerilla Family, Black Liberation Army members and Puerto Rican Independence groups, etc. etc.) instead, almost from the outset, the state sought to intertwine criminal prison-based organizations, street gangs and organized crime outfits with these Revolutionary formations within their criminological lexicon, characterizing all of them as "gangs" – or more recently, "Security Threat Groups" (STG's). This, like every aspect of their domestic torture program, was a calculated measure. Here the staff sought to criminalize legitimate Revolutionary formations and political progressives through the simple turn of a phrase; a strategic act of libel and slander encoded into their very regulations on gang "validation" and indeterminate SHU confinement. In an instant, anyone "validated" as a "gang member" by "law" became a gang member, no matter if they were a Political Prisoner or a political gangster. This served a dual purpose; it dehumanized anyone the state labeled a "gang member" in the eyes of the public, while providing a false basis for the denial of the existence of Political Prisoners in Amerika, made plausible by three decades of PISC lobbying and media propaganda. This recasting of progressive political ideologues as "gang members," acts as a manufactured regulatory loophole, which allows CDC(r) officials to interfere with and blatantly repress the Constitutional rights of these Prisoners (see U.S.C. 1st Amendment, etc.) via threats, intimidation and coercion under color of law; an equally blatant violation of state and federal hate crime statutes.

That CDC(r) has used the distance of these torture units as a means to influence public opinion in support of prison expansion and draconian sentencing laws is further evidence of the subversion of justice to advance the particular economic interests of CDC(r) employees engaged in this racketeering enterprise. This century long pattern, practice and expansion of the use of domestic torture units, and the use of systemic torture techniques to coerce information (from) and retaliate against Political Prisoners for exercising their Constitutional rights, all in furtherance of an ongoing racketeering enterprise violates Title 18 s1961, s1952; U.S.C. 1st Amendment, 8th Amendment and 14th Amendment; Civil Code s52.1, Government Code s11135, s8.12; Penal Code s422.77 and Title 18 s2340.

INDICTMENT COUNT 6:

CONSPIRACY TO EXTORT, EMBEZZLE, MISAPPROPRIATE AND LAUNDER FUNDS OBTAINED VIA AN ONGOING CRIMINAL ENTERPRISE.

CDC(r) is engaged in a pattern and practice of extortionate money transactions relating to the collection of restitution (which is not going to victims), retention of interest earned on Prisoner trust accounts (without the authorization, and in most cases without the knowledge, of Prisoner account holders), and misappropriating an additional 10% on all restitution and other transactions (with the exception of canteen draws).

As part of the annual budget, funds are allotted to CDC(r) trust offices to conduct all financial transactions and maintain Prisoner trust accounts. However, with the introduction of mandatory restitution fines and CDC(r)'s voluntary collection of ever increasing percentages (from 22% to the current 55%) of those fines from funds sent to Prisoners by their Families and Friends (outside of prison "wages"), CDC(r) has begun to unilaterally extort an additional 10% of the amount of every transaction, be it a restitution fine or special purchase, ostensibly to cover "transaction costs."

Being that the California General Fund already allots all CDC(r) facilities appropriate funding to cover all its operations (which include "transaction costs"), the stated purpose of these appropriations is fictitious, and instead CDC(r) is embezzling a percentage of the funds Prisoner's friends and families are sending them to line their pockets (much like Sheriffs did when skimming off the top of food funds allotted for people victimized by convict leasing, thereby starving their charges). To be sure, the trust accounts for each Prisoner are themselves interest earning accounts, and the interest incurred, by right, should go to the Prisoners themselves. Yet, since the very inception of the trust account system, CDC(r) has been kicking that interest back to themselves, padding its budget to cover exorbitant overtime costs. These embezzled funds are then illegally transferred to CDC(r) accounts based on the compounding interest schedule of the bank(s).

If it is a Prisoner's position that they do not want to give CDC(r) 10% of their funds on each transaction, CDC(r) will simply refuse to process the transaction at all, in effect coercing Prisoners into giving up the 10% when the state has already allocated funding for that purpose. This constitutes both extortion and embezzlement.

CDC(r) is also the primary agent in the state's ongoing misappropriation of funds sent from Friends and Family to Prisoners. No restitution order has been levied against these citizens, yet every time they send funds to their imprisoned loved ones who may have a restitution order CDC(r) takes 55% of it; 50% they kick to the state and 5% they keep themselves (10% of that 50%), in a scheme which not only targets the funds of Friends and Family of the subject Prisoner, but also have no intention of using those funds for the reasons stated. CDC(r) and the state claim funds appropriated from Prisoners accounts goes to "victims' restitution," however, they do not. Instead those funds are allotted to a cabal of special interest groups, some of them Victims' Rights Organizations and state law enforcement agencies, not the actual victims of crimes. To be sure, there are many offenses, such as drug possession or possession of a weapon in prison, which have no victims at all for which the courts levy exorbitant restitution fines in furtherance of this racketeering enterprise. Most victims of crime are from the very communities that the offenders are from, and in the case of "gang" related offenses, often the victim is another gang member, occasionally under some form of correctional control themselves. In most cases, none of these victims see a dime of this money; instead these funds remain under state control to be used to enrich its municipalities, like CDC(r).

This engagement in monetary transactions in funds derived from extortion, embezzlement and misappropriation of funds, and doing so utilizing the financial mechanisms of the public trust constitutes one of the most egregious instances of state sanctioned money laundering perhaps in U.S. history. This pattern and practice of fraudulent and illegal misappropriation, embezzlement, money laundering and extortions constitutes an ongoing racketeering enterprise in violation of Title 18 s1952, s1956, s1957, s1960, s1961, s664, s891-894, s1341, s1343, s1344 of the United States Code.

INDICTMENT COUNT 7:

SLAVERY AND TRAFFICKING IN PERSONS.

CDC(r) has engaged in a pattern and practice of de-facto commoditization of criminal offenders and farming out prison contracts to private prison operators both in California and out of state. In all cases of imprisonments in the U.S. (like those subject to the custody of CDC(r)) citizenship is effectively stripped by, and through, the 13th Amendment to the U.S. Constitution. Prisoners are subject to "involuntary servitude" and are by legal definition – slaves.

Prisoners cannot "strike" to protest inhumane treatment, cannot vote, cannot freely pursue their political, religious or social expression without the regulation or express permission of the state. CDC(r), and its political proxy the CCPOA, has taken this concept to new levels of profiteering, by assigning a specific dollar amount to each prisoner based on their custody level and the institution they're housed in. In California, if you are housed in G.P. (General population), CDC(r) (as of fiscal year 2020 & 2021) receives an average of $106,000 a year per prisoner; for Ad-seg and SHU $127,000 per prisoner; and for those housed in the SHU "Short Corridor" or other "High Power" units $135,000 per prisoner annually. Of course, it only costs a fraction of this, between $8K and $15K per year (depending on the health of the prisoner) to feed, clothe, house and confine a prisoner in a concrete box annually, the rest goes to enrich CDC(r) officers, officials, contractors, medical staff, private prisons or their corporate suppliers (including medical services companies).

To ensure the exorbitant multi-billion dollar operating budget continues to flow from the general fund, CDCr carries out a carefully orchestrated political influence and public propaganda campaign to ensure passage (and ongoing public support) for some of the most draconian mandatory minimum laws and sentencing statutes in the U.S. over the past 30 years. In a 20 year span (from 1985-2005) the CDCr prisoner population expanded by 800%. This includes their juvenile corrections division, the California Youth Authority.

CDCr officers are the highest paid correctional officers in Amerika (aka Amerikkka); with base salaries starting at $68,000, plus benefits and average annual pay of $98,000 a year. To be sure, though crime rates have been on a continuous downward slide for the past 25 years, prison populations have only increased as had CDCr's share of the general fund.

For example in fiscal year 2015-2016 CDC(r)'s portion of the general fund rose by 1.7% from $9.955 Billion to $10.16 Billion, while overall state spending only rose 1.4%; demonstrating CDC(r) spending is increasing faster than the budget average. To be sure, CDC(r) was allotted an additional $2.516 Billion in special funds bringing their actual budget up to $12.676 Billion of your tax dollars. This is not counting the funding the state set aside for 15,892 beds leased from private prison corporations both in California and out of state (from GEO Group and Correctional Corporation of America), not to mention the additional funds to expand new beds in existing facilities. In spite of this, CDC(r) is currently operating with a total prisoner population over 141.5% of its designed capacity; all of this in the face of "realignment" and passage of multiple "propositions" [Prop 26, Prop 47, Prop 57, etc.] designed to decrease the prisoner population. [Source: Californians United for a Responsible Budget, 2015/2016].

These exorbitant salaries, vastly increased by routine overtime hustling by staff (with overtime pay correctional officers can average $98-$120 thousands a year), are based on a single premise; the number of humans under correctional control at any given time determines how much or how little of the general fund CDC(r) can appropriate. The more humans they have in chains, the more money they control. The prison industrial slave complex (PISC) is just that – an industry based on the legalization of human bondage – a collusion of state and corporate interests who have utilized their political influence in the legislative and judicial branches of the state to target specific populations (the prison population is overwhelmingly New Afrikan(Black), Latinos, and the poor) for criminalization and legal enslavement through mass incarceration with their primary motive force being their economic enrichment and the maximization of their political power.

Though slavery and trafficking in persons is prohibited under Title 18 U.S.C. S1581-s1592 it is permissible for those convicted of a felony, under the 13th Amendment to the U.S. Constitution, creating a "legal" slavery provision for those communities and populations subject to criminalization via C.C.P.O.A influenced policies and legislation. The fact that slavery and involuntary servitude have not been expressly prohibited for ALL populations under U.S. law is the best proof of the willful collusion of state and corporate interests in this criminal enterprise. They provide the state with an effective social control mechanism (mass incarceration), while acting as an influential base of political support for politicians amicable to their agenda (albeit an artificially manufactured political base of prison guards, employees and their family members). In return, the state allows CDC(r) and their corporate partners to run this racket on the backs of Black, Brown and Poor People unmolested and under color of law. That prisoners offset the operation costs of running these facilities by providing compulsory labor in almost every aspect of operation goes without saying, as involuntary servitude is a standard component of slavery.

This pattern and practice of modern day slavery and trafficking in persons, though permissible under U.S. law (see U.S.C. 13th Amendment, 1st), is never the less in violation of both the letter and language of the law articulated in Title 18 U.S.C. S1961, s1952, s1581-s1592, and s1957. This racket constitutes perhaps the greatest conflict of interest in U.S. history; those the people have invested with the responsibility for their public safety have their economic interests tied to maximizing the number of "criminal" offenders under their control, thus the number of crimes committed, and have used these ill-gotten gains to influence legislation and judicial appointments to expand the list of things which are a "crime" and deepen the penalty for them, all to enrich themselves and expand their industry's share of the public product (tax dollars). This clear violation of the R.I.C.O. Act constitutes a clear and present danger to public safety and welfare; and among the most egregious offenses one can commit under color of law.

INDICTMENT COUNT 8:

CONSPIRACY TO DENY NEW AFRIKAN POLITICAL/POLITICIZED PRISONERS FREE ENJOYMENT OF CONSTITUTIONALLY PROTECTED EXPRESSION/ACTIVITY THROUGH LIBEL, SLANDER, RETALIATION, DISCRIMINATION, PERJURY AND THE PREPARATION OF FALSE DOCUMENTS.

CDC(r) has been engaged in a pattern and practice of illegal discrimination and denial of constitutionally protected rights (U.S.C. 1st Amen. etc.) directed against New Afrikan Political and Politicized Prisoners through a campaign of slander, libel and retaliation which includes the preparation of false documents and perjury.

For decades, leading up to 2015, CDC(r) has specifically targeted New Afrikan Political and Politicized Prisoners, their associates, ideas, books, literature, language, correspondence and even their very history for slanderous and libelous characterizations as "gang members", gang material and/or gang activity in order to justify unprecedented retaliation which includes everything from extreme censorship to indefinite solitary confinement.

CDC(r), and to a large extent the U.S. government itself (Department of Homeland Security, law enforcement agencies, correctional lobbies, etc.), have waged an over 40 year campaign to dehumanize most anyone the state has characterized as "Gangs" or "Gang Members." The state has become adept at utilizing such defamatory labels to delegitimize and/or criminalize transformative political opposition which exposes its core contradictions, especially when that opposition is New Afrikan or Revolutionary in form. This is standard U.S. State practice.

For example, in 1968 the Chicago police department, in conjunction with the F.B.I., developed an entirely new "Gang Task Force" that, in spite of having several of the largest and most notorious gangs in the U.S. operating in the city (according to them), had a single target: The Black Panther Party (which, of course, was not a "Gang"). CDC(r) took this model to an entirely new level when it not only began to identify imprisoned New Afrikan Revolutionary Nationalist (NARN) and their associates as "gang members," but then utilized this defamatory characterization to subject them to the full force of state sanctions.

The terms "Gang" or "Security Threat group" (STG's) automatically elicits images in the public's mind of predatory criminal groups, plotting how best to prey on others. The great irony here is New Afrikan Revolutionary Nationalists (NARN) who has been falsely labeled "Gang Members" or "Gang associates" are themselves dedicated to transforming the New Afrikan (Black) criminal mentality into a New Afrikan progressive mentality, to finding solutions to Gang violence and alternatives to the survival activities of desperately poor communities. To be sure, the language of CDCr's "STG management policy" contends, "California security threat groups (STG's) are routinely and consistently connected to major criminal activities in communities, including such crimes as homicides, drug trafficking, human trafficking and extortion…(STG's) are largely responsible for criminal activities within institutions, to include the trafficking of narcotics, committing and/or directing violence...and directing criminal activities."

However, New Afrikan Revolutionary Nationalists (NARN) in California have never been indicted for a single criminal act, and it is well documented by CDC(r)'s Institutional Gang Investigators (IGI) themselves that California imprisoned NARN activists are anti-drug use/or trafficking, anti-prostitution, anti-human trafficking, anti-extortion and anti-criminal activity, something the drafters of the CDC(r) STG management policy are fully aware of.

The primary purpose of this lie is to criminalize legitimate New Afrikan leftist Political activism within the California prison system, and to prevent its resonance within broader society. To be sure, within the same 'STG management policy', CDC(r) developed a "STG disciplinary matrix" dedicated to elevating innocuous, non-criminal activities and matter to the level of "criminal STG behavior." This "Disciplinary matrix" (CCR Title 15 s3378.4) criminalizes "conversations," "Greeting Cards," "clothing," "communications with offenders/others," "Group Exercise," "Handshakes," "Artwork," and, believe it or not, a "Color." S3378.2(7) allows for staff visual and audible observations of "STG Offenses" for which you will be punished.

The 1st Amendment to the U.S. Constitution states, "Congress shall make no law...abridging the freedom of speech....", yet that's precisely what CDC(r) has done, and employed overt defamation to carry this out. We could go on for pages, but the question is already clear: Why would CDC(r)'s public propaganda hype these serious and violent crimes as the focus of state interest when their policy itself focuses primarily on criminalizing things which are, in fact, not crimes? The answer is fairly obvious: Those NARN Prisoners CDC(r) has falsely labeled "gang members" are, in fact, anti-crime, and have done nothing at all save express their political ideas, so CDC(r) must manufacture a basis to criminalize them. NARN Prisoners are no more "gang members" than lions are wolves, and CDC(r) knows this. It's an absurdity made more absurd by CDC(r)'s continued attempts to justify it.

Defamation is "the unlawful act of intentionally speaking (slander) or printing (libel) false and/or unjustifiable statements designed to injure the reputation and/or public perception of an individual or group." Clearly NARN Prisoners confined to CDC(r) have been subject to systematic defamation. This pattern and practice of defamation against New Afrikan Revolutionary Nationalists in California Prisons is then exacerbated by the greater offense of discrimination via threats, violence, torture and 1st Amendment retaliation. CDC(r) has engaged in a pattern of manufacturing false and misleading narratives to defame the character(s) of principled NARN Prisoners (in violation of their own regulations prohibiting discrimination by race, religion, nationality and political belief), then punish the victim of that crime by subjecting them to denial of their 1st Amendment rights, political repression, racial discrimination, indefinite solitary confinement, retaliation for exercising their 1st Amendment rights, assault and even murder.

That these libelous claims were entered into official state records in numerous documents from CDC(r) classification and validation chronos to investigative memos, to trial proceedings, they constitute both preparation and offering of false evidence in violation of Penal Code s134, s132 and s115. Because CDC(r) officials have relied on a pattern and practice of employing coerced confidential informants (most often those who've "debriefed" after being threatened with, or subjected to, indefinite solitary confinement) to bolster their defamatory claims in investigatory documents and court proceedings, they are responsible for both committing perjury and suborning perjury. To be sure, as previously demonstrated, CDC(r)'s own regulations conflict with themselves on the basis of discrimination, demonstrating not simply a propensity to subordinate their adherence to these regulations prohibiting discrimination, to their need to further their ongoing conspiracy to deny NARN Prisoners the free enjoyment of their constitutional rights, but their deliberation in carrying out these crimes as well. CDC(r) Title 15 s3004 mandates all Prisoners "have the right to be treated respectfully, impartially and fairly by all employees," and will "not be subjected to any form of discrimination based on race, nationality or political belief"; yet s3023 and s3378.2 provide a virtually limitless "regulatory" basis to do just the opposite under the guise of "STG interdiction."

Though there are thousands of cases of CDC(r) utilizing "Gang" suppression regulations to commit crimes against New Afrikan Revolutionary Nationalist Prisoners, we can find not one documented case where prison officials have invoked s3004 to prevent such abuses.

That the primary intent of this ongoing criminal mischaracterization is the maintenance of the false narrative that there exists a universal prevalence of predatory gangs (fraudulently including NARN Prisoners) as the basis upon which the Prison Industrial Slave Complex justifies their appropriation of these exorbitant portions of Public money, is some of the best proof we have that it is indeed an overarching conspiracy and establishes a direct link to the overall racketeering enterprise. This pattern and practice of defamatory discrimination and perjury in furtherance of a criminal enterprise violates Title 18 U.S.C. 1st Amen., U.S.C. 8th Amen., Civil Code 52, Civil Code s8.12, Government Code s11135, s11139, P.C. s132, P.C. s134, P.C. s127, P.C. s115, U.S.C. Title 18 s1512 and s1513.

INDICTMENT COUNT 9:

UNLAWFUL IMPRISONMENT.

The policy of the California Board of Parole Hearings which denies release to Prisoners long beyond their base terms until they are infirmed, chronically ill or dead constitutes a violation of the inalienable rights to "life, liberty and the pursuit of happiness" guaranteed under U.S. law.

The function of true "Justice" in any society is the upholding of human rights transferred to a common power apex through the mutual agreement of the People's subject to the mechanisms of that Justice. The historic legacy of economically exploiting human bondage in the United States stretches in an unbroken line from the chattel slavery era, to the perpetuation of slavery beyond Reconstruction enshrined in the exception clause of the 13th Amendment, on to the industrialization of prisons and imprisonment we know today as mass incarceration and the Prison Industrial Slave-Complex (PISC).

Cannon to U.S. Law is the inalienable right to "Life, Liberty and the Pursuit of Happiness," however these inalienable "rights" are routinely denied to the indeterminately sentenced Prisoner class in the U.S. in general, and the state of California in particular. As a matter of policy, the Board of Parole Hearings (BPH) denies parole to members of the Indeterminate Class far beyond they're base term, even when it is clear they are no threat to public safety, completely divorcing this crucial component of corrections (parole) from the inalienable rights of "life, liberty and the pursuit of happiness" promised to all under U.S. law. Once so sentenced, the economic interests of the U.S. Prison Industrial Slave-Complex take precedence over these so-called "rights." Indeterminate Sentence Class Prisoners are denied parole, repeatedly for the most facile reasons until they either die, are killed or are so sick, old and infirmed that there is no quality of life to speak of. In case after case, most can barely walk, let alone pursue happiness of any meaningful sort. Of the many mechanisms of the U.S. judicial machinery and PISC presiding over this denial of rights, the single most influential body in this process is THE BOARD OF PAROLE HEARINGS.

This draconian policy of holding Indeterminate Sentence Class prisoners long beyond any public safety concern solely to maximize the number of human commodities under their correctional control costs society much more than the billions of dollars flowing into correctional budgets. The exorbitant cost of maintaining the health care of an ageing Indeterminate Sentence Class is perhaps the single largest burden on state budgets outside of Prison Guard salaries and benefits themselves. Though the National annual healthcare costs per prisoner stands at approximately $7000 per inmate, California averages $12,442 per inmate. This is primarily due to the inflated number of Indeterminate Sentence Class prisoners over 50 in the state of California, clearly a deliberate degradation to the right to "life, liberty and pursuit of happiness." 26% of all annual incarceration costs go to healthcare. According to the California Finance Department it costs an average of $106,000 per year to incarcerate a prisoner in California. About three quarters of these costs are for security and healthcare; Security being prison guard salaries. Since 2010-2011 the cost of incarceration has risen by $57,000 per prisoner annually or about 117%.

Maintaining the imprisonment of a single prisoner in California now costs more than a year of tuition at Harvard. Though the base pay of California Correctional officers averages around $68,070 a year (the highest pay in the nation), the rampant exploitation of overtime rates at most every prison in the state places the true average salary at around $98,000 annually.

Though the 21 Commissioners of the Board of Parole Hearings are selected by the Governor and confirmed by the state Senate, it is the political lobbying of the CCPOA, the plethora of corporations that hold contracts for prisons and their special interest groups which influence the election of members to the Senate, and all too often the Governor's office itself, thus holding sway over the composition of Parole Boards themselves. With an average annual salary of $81,250 a year, Parole Board members have a strong economic motivation to maintain this racket. However, even more disturbing, and central to this argument, is the overt dehumanization of the

Indeterminate Sentence Class by both Parole Boards and correctional administrators necessary to deny them the right to "life, liberty and the pursuit of happiness" year after year. This process of dehumanization, perhaps more than anything else, demonstrates why it is essential that new mechanisms for determining parole grants and suitability must be considered by the People.

Current parole boards are composed of former police, district attorneys, former judges and other law enforcement professionals who do NOT live, work and in most instances have never seen the Communities from which those subject to their decisions come from. Yet they interpret the values and social experiences of these Communities, and those who hail from them, through the prism of static, all too often contradictory, psych evaluations and the values of their own ultra-conservative, right wing world view, absolving social policy and social conditions of any role in the offenders manner of thinking and activities; an absurd decision making framework in the context of determining the probability of an ongoing public safety threat.

The ultra-conservative nature of representative governance in the U.S. has created a political climate of permissive special interest which is NOT representative of the People's will and or their interests. The U.S. judicial machinery has successfully morphed into a multi-billion dollar racket using the poor and disenfranchised as a commodity to extort billions of dollars from Our state's general fund.

We should all be disturbed that the U.S., and the state of California in particular, have presided over the single largest prison population on Earth, with policies of mass incarceration which have devastated poor Communities across America, fractured family units, exacerbated generational poverty and facilitated the school to poverty to prison pipeline, even though crime rates have been on a steady decline over the past 25 years. It doesn't make us safe, diverts money from viable Initiatives that could, and enriches an exclusive industry at the expense of Our entire society.

To be sure, in the 1970's, just prior to the expansion of the PISC following the decimation of the Black Liberation Movement through the Counter Intelligence Program (COINTELPRO), the statutory definition of "life" imprisonment in the state of California was 20 years. The Bureau of Justice Statistics finds that those who are 50 years or older or who have served 20 years or more of continuous confinement have a .015% recidivism rate; virtually non-existent. The Indeterminate Sentence Class Prisoner, before becoming eligible for parole, must serve his/her minimum base term, often the number of years immediately preceding "to life" (i.e. 15 to life, 20 to life, 25 to life, etc.). Both by previous historical precedent and empirical data, the Indeterminate Sentence Class Prisoner is by far the single safest cohort of Prisoners that can be released from prison.

However, since the bloated expansion of the PISC in California (an expansion of 800% since the 1970's) one early release scheme after another (purportedly to relieve overcrowding) has focused primarily on "non-violent drug offenders" a cohort of Prisoners with one of the single largest recidivism rates in the state; 70%. Why would CDCr and the Parole Department knowingly deny release to the safest cohort of Prisoners in favor of the most criminally inclined if their motivation was not to maintain a high incarceration rate in order to maximize their own economic security and political influence? The short answer is they wouldn't.

In light of the previous 8 counts of this Indictment, Count 9 cannot be viewed in isolation, but must be viewed in light of its interconnection to this extensive pattern of criminal conduct. This is not a mere matter of a deferred liberty interest in parole for criminal offenders, but instead a systematic policy of denying release to Prisoners who have both served their time and pose no threat to public safety in order to pad their industries guaranteed allotment of funds, and as a political tool to use to extort even more financial and political concessions in the future. It is a form of unlawful imprisonment which rises to the level of kidnapping under color of law, for to hold a prisoner who has served their time and poses no threat to public safety solely as an economic instrument is nothing short of kidnapping. This pattern and practice of intentionally and systematically denying parole to Indeterminate Sentence Class Prisoners long after they would be otherwise released, to maintain a significant base prisoner commodity population as a means to facilitate an ongoing racket stands in violation of PC 207; PC 236; and 18 USC 1959; 18 USC 241 & 242.

CONCLUSION

The California Department of Corrections and Rehabilitation, for purposes of the RICO Act is clearly a racket, and in the face of the long standing and pervasive nature of this racketeering activity, it is clear that the existing system of "justice" either has no interest in prosecuting such an Indictment, or is itself complicit in the racket we know as the PISC.

To be sure, 42 USC 1983 would be one of the vehicles employed by the People, in the normal course of affairs, to redress violations of their rights by state actors; however, U.S. law is designed to shield state crimes against the People from redress. Restrictive statutes of limitations, the Heck bar, qualified immunity statutes, unreasonable evidentiary standards and exorbitant filing fees all serve to protect state actors from liability in such actions. The RICO Act is specifically designed to address such long standing corrupt enterprises, especially when they have successfully corrupted the normal processes of governance.

The California Department of Corrections and rehabilitation (CDCr) in conjunction with the California Correctional Peace Officers Association (CCPOA) and California Parole Department functions like a mob, utilizing Prisoners, Parolees and the contradictions these state actors have manufactured within prisons to reduce poor People consigned to their custody to commodities allowing them to extort billions of dollars from the general fund and kickbacks from corporate contractors.

Some legal scholars will balk at the use of RICO against a municipality, (in spite of its laundry list of indictable acts), asserting that, much like 42 USC 1983 there are too many procedural fatalities. But, the law would disagree.

Nothing in RICO civil or criminal jurisprudence suggests that it cannot, or should not, be applied to Law Enforcement, Correctional or any other state actors. To be sure, in Sedima, S.P.R.I. v. Imrex Co. and subsequent legislation the Supreme Court has maintained, RICO applies to ANYONE in violation of its statutes; and the legislative intent of RICO is virtually tailor made to prosecute such corruption. RICO has been applied to white collar criminal enterprises extensively, even though many legal professionals argue its application to security's fraud and other such criminal acts was not its intent; in contrast, the racketeering activity of the CDCr and its affiliates much more closely resembles the criminal enterprises of the traditional mob. The human misery resultant from CDCr's racket is borne, by and large, by 2 primary victims: 1) the prisoners being commoditized in this racket and their Communities (almost exclusively poor and minority Communities) and 2) the People of the State of California (whose tax dollars fuel this criminal enterprise).

The former lack the political influence and economic resources to combat an entrenched industrial interest which enjoys the perceived legitimacy of law enforcement like the CDCr, while the latter are wholly oblivious that a racket is even being perpetrated, let alone that they are being victimized by said criminal enterprise. Because decades of dehumanizing rhetoric has essentially reduced criminal offenders (and their Communities) to non-persons in the minds of most in this society, the perpetrators of this racket bear a degree of shielding from the belief systems of a large swathe of their victims; the People of the State of California (and the U.S. at large) themselves. Even in the face of the overwhelming evidence presented herein, some of you reading this now will find it difficult to align your interests with prisoners and criminal offenders that you have been convinced are sub humans. It is perhaps one of the greatest defenses CDCr has enjoyed in expanding this racket over the span of decades with no fear of exposure or intervention by – anyone. So long as PISC corrupt practices remain primarily the problem of People of color and the poor, they are confident political action will not yield any meaningful adverse consequences for them or their activities. It is this confidence in the unassailability of their racket which makes the RICO, not only the appropriate vehicle for redress, but the ONLY legal action with any hope of meaningful and lasting change.

For purposes of the RICO Act the enterprise carrying out the racket must be distinct. The CDCr and its affiliates is clearly the enterprise by which the PISC racket was devised, while its many officers and affiliated staff (represented by and large by the CCPOA) are the conductors of this enterprise, or otherwise known as the "defendants."

Under RICO the corrupt enterprise must "affect interstate commerce." Obviously the management and oversight of the imprisonment and release of criminal offenders will influence the growth and development of business, tourism and home ownership in a state, all of which impact interstate commerce.

However, it is the manipulation and commoditization of prisoners and imprisonment which allows them the tacit justification to defer ever larger portions of the state's general fund (which could be deferred to other legitimate enterprises) which unquestioningly adversely impacts interstate commerce between the State of California and the rest of the nation (and world). Because we have so clearly outlined the predicate offenses listed in the RICO Act and the unambiguous relationship between the enterprise and these prohibited activities, we need not explore these standards here, as to do so would be redundant. However, to be cognizable under the

RICO Act there must be a clearly established "pattern of racketeering activity."

The CDCr and its affiliates, as we've outlined here in each count, has had as its primary or secondary motivation, 3 primary goals: 1) Maintain a high prison population and recidivism rates; 2) Ensure the economic resources to maintain undue influence in the makeup of those legislative and political entities impacting their access to the state's general fund and sole oversight of corporate contracts to supply and construct prisons; 3) Maintain exorbitant salary and benefit packages for their members constituting a recession proof labor aristocracy and perpetual job security. This racket has gone on and expanded over the course of decades, statistically documented in the expansion of the prison population by 800% over the course of the last 30 years. To be sure, since FY 2010-2011, the cost of incarceration has increased by $57,000 or about 117%. At a cost of over $106,000 per year per prisoner, it now costs more to lock up a prisoner in California than it does for a year's tuition at Harvard; $98,000 a year on average going to prison guard pay. This combination of the inextricable relationship between these corrupt practices and criminal acts, and their continuation over so long a time constitutes the pattern of racketeering activity demanded by the statute.

The RICO Act confines its injury showing, in traditional U.S. capitalist fashion, to "business or property." Human injuries to life, liberty, relationships, etc., are for purpose of RICO confined to the predicate offenses, not the RICO Act itself. In spite of the conflicting opinions between the 9th Circuit's ruling in Oscar v. University Students Cooperative Association (which held that injury under RICO requires concrete financial loss and not mere injury to "a valuable intangible property interest") and the 5th Circuit's ruling in Khurana v. Innovative Health Care Systems, Inc. (which held that damages to both professional reputation and lost business/employment opportunities were cognizable injuries under RICO), there is no definitive determination on what constitutes injury under RICO. However, considering the nature of this particular racket which has so definitively impacted so many lives, from successfully lobbying to bar prisoners from engaging in any form of business activity or employment outside of slave labor to the multitude of collateral consequences of imprisonment upon release (from diminished employment opportunities to the barring of former felons from gaining over 200 different professional licenses, public housing, etc.) suffered by parolees and their Communities, to the diminished economic investment by the state (due to funds for social services and economic empowerment programs being deferred to prison budgets) in poor Communities, the economic injury suffered by the imprisoned and the People is incalculable.

With all of this in mind, the application of the RICO Act to the ongoing criminal enterprise of the CDCr and its Prison Industrial Slave Complex is implied in the very purpose of the Act itself. The legislative intent of the RICO is 3 fold:

1) To stop the destructive impact of organized crime on the U.S. economy; 2) To prevent the infiltration of criminals into legitimate enterprises; 3) To give those victimized by the racketeering activity of an ongoing criminal enterprise a way to gain Restitution for those injuries.

The Courts have already ruled definitively that the RICO is not reserved for known mobs alone, but ANYONE who violates its statutes. In this instance the historical inclination of U.S. industry to monetize the mechanisms of human bondage began in the chattel slave era was simply modernized and continued. Viewing objectively the nature of U.S. capitalism in conjunction with the function of Corrections, legislators, laws and social policies governing human bondage where reviewed over time then corrupted where they were not maximizing that exploitation, in a process that was as inevitable as juice turning into vinegar over time. Both the actions (murder, drug trafficking, slavery, etc.) and inactions (failure to dismiss or arrest those responsible for cultivating this monolithic prison expansion into the multi-billion dollar racket it has become) has no doubt had an impact on the economic life of the state of California and America in general.

In terms of defending legitimate enterprises from infiltration by criminal actors, as I said at the outset, the modern PISC is perhaps the greatest conflict of interest in U.S. history; those responsible for maintaining public safety have their economic and political interests tied to maximizing the number of criminal offenders under their correctional control at any given time. I can think of no more salient application of the RICO in this regard than seeking to preserve the legitimacy of the public safety function of the correctional and parole machinery in the state.

Finally, redress for both private and public injuries suffered by prisoners and the People resulting from prohibited racketeering activity are precisely what the RICO was designed to accomplish. Therefore, it is clear this Indictment against CDCr, the state and its Prison Industrial Slave-Complex is both factual and legally cognizable. One universal fact about the function of RICO is its targets tend to be institutions and enterprises so enormous and influential that their power to negatively affect the lives of the People is often monstrous in its scope. The RICO then provides the People with a means to fight back, to at least socially and politically expose the racket to the light of day. There exists no greater disproportion in power than an oppressed minority population in opposition to an institution imbued with the power to deprive most anyone of their freedom.

Do you not grasp the insidious nature of this criminal enterprise? Do you not see the far reaching implications of a corrupt PISC, functioning with virtually no oversight? There exists no organized crime outfit you can name that has ever possessed the 2 things the CDCr and its Prison Industrial Slave-Complex enjoy: 1) the perception of legitimacy in the minds of the masses and 2) the full backing of the U.S. Government. If ever there was an instance where it was necessary that we the People sought to prosecute a RICO Indictment against an entrenched industrial enterprise, it is this one.

If we fail to either break this racket or restructure the processes of the correctional and judicial machinery currently making up the PISC, we will all ultimately be subject to the absolute despotism of state run rackets exploiting the very enterprises upon which society is based – or has that already occurred? As outlined in the beginning of this Indictment, and throughout its predicate offenses, it was shown that the judicial machinery was either reluctant to intervene, actually complicit in allowing the racket to continue, or interpreted the law in such a way that it actually shields the racket from the consequences of its activity. In such a state of affairs, it may well be prudent that we take steps now to forge new institutions, independent of these corrupted enterprises. In the final analysis what YOU, the People, do with this Indictment will determine the character of this society, whether it is a Nation striving towards justice or a slave state that has legitimized larceny and murder under color of law.

Your action – or inaction – will determine which.

Presented on behalf of the NCTT and the People